DRUMMER BOYS
LEAD THE CHARGE

Courageous Kids of the Civil War

by Bruce Berglund

illustrated by Aleksandar Sotirovski

Consultant:
Tim Solie
Adjunct Professor of History
Minnesota State University, Mankato
Mankato, Minnesota

T0081174

CAPSTONE PRESS
a capstone imprint

Graphic Library is published by Capstone Press, an imprint of Capstone.
1710 Roe Crest Drive, North Mankato, Minnesota 56003
www.capstonepub.com

Library of Congress Cataloging-in-Publication data is available
at the Library of Congress wesite.
ISBN: 978-1-4966-8504-9 (library binding)
ISBN: 978-1-4966-8805-7 (paperback)
ISBN: 978-1-4966-8508-7 (eBook PDF)

Summary: In the early 1860s, the United States is torn apart by Civil War. The conflict affects everyone, including many boys who want to join the fight. Among them are young Edward Black, Lyston and Orion Howe, and Miles Moore. They're too young to fight in battle, but show their courage by marching as drummer boys. Despite the risk of being wounded, captured, or even killed in action, they bravely face the danger to fight for their country.

INTERIOR INKING AND COLORING
Aleksandar Sotirovski,
Adrienn Schönberg, Barbara Gyuricza,
István Attila Szabó, Martyn Cain,
Moreno Chiacchiera, Nadene Naude
(Beehive Illustration)

ART DIRECTOR
Nathan Gassman

EDITOR
Aaron J. Sautter

DESIGNER
Ted Williams

MEDIA RESEARCHER
Morgan Walters

PRODUCTION SPECIALIST
Laura Manthe

Direct quotations appear in **bold italicized text** on the following pages:

Pages 9, 13: from *The Indiana Jackass Regiment: A History of the 21st Infantry/1st Heavy Artillery Regiment,* by Philip E. Faller. Jefferson, NC: McFarland, 2013.
Page 22: from "Men of Color: To Arms!" by Frederick Douglass, *Broadside,* Rochester, March 21, 1863. University of Rochester Frederick Douglass Project, https://rbscp.lib.rochester. edu/4372.

Printed and bound in the United states of America.
PA117

TABLE OF CONTENTS

THE BEAT OF A DRUM

In 1861 Americans went to war against each other. Leaders of Southern states broke away to form their own country, the Confederate States of America. They believed that U.S. President Abraham Lincoln was going to limit their rights to own slaves. Many people in the North felt that the states had to stay together. They fought to preserve the Union.

The Civil War between the Northern and Southern states lasted four bloody years. More than two million soldiers fought in the Union and Confederate armies.

By the time the war ended in 1865, more than 600,000 soldiers were killed—more than in any other war in American history.

In the middle of this terrible war were many young boys. They served alongside soldiers as drummer boys.

The drummer boys didn't just play marching music. Their drums were also important for communications in battle.

Hold your line, men!

BOOM!

RAT TA-TAT! RAT TA-TAT! RAT-TA-TAT!

In the Civil War, there were no radios or phones. Soldiers could not hear their orders over the noise of the battlefield. The different drum beats told them what they had to do.

Drummers played many combinations of beats. Soldiers knew what each combination meant— march or run, turn left or right, charge or retreat.

To the bridge!

Let's move it, men! Double quick!

Drummer boys were the youngest soldiers in the army. But they had to show incredible courage on the battlefield. The soldiers depended on them to know where to go and how to fight.

BRRRR-RUM-PUM-RUM! BRRRR-RUM-PUM-RUM!

THE YOUNGEST DRUMMER BOY

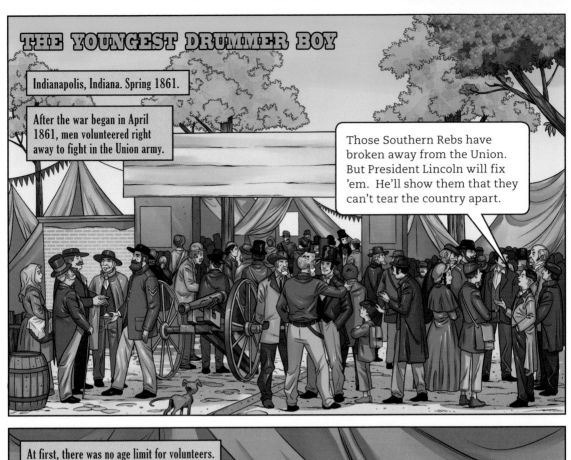

Indianapolis, Indiana. Spring 1861.

After the war began in April 1861, men volunteered right away to fight in the Union army.

Those Southern Rebs have broken away from the Union. But President Lincoln will fix 'em. He'll show them that they can't tear the country apart.

At first, there was no age limit for volunteers.

Where you boys from?

We're from Fort Wayne, sir. Walked more than 100 miles.

How old are you?

I'll be 15 years in October, sir. My two cousins here are 13 and 14.

Hundreds of thousands of teenage boys served in both the Union and Confederate armies.

Edward Black volunteered for the 21st Indiana Regiment when he was only 8 years old.

We need drummers for the regiment. Are you up for that?

I'm a hard worker, sir. I'll do what you ask.

At first, life in the army was no adventure.

This is just like doing chores back home on the farm.

I wonder when we're going to fight the Rebs.

The volunteers did not have uniforms or muskets. First, they had to learn how to be soldiers.

Prepare to march at my command! Count your steps to the drum! Ready . . .

After weeks of training, the 21st Indiana Regiment was ready for service.

Edward was now Private Black, Musician Third Class—the youngest soldier to serve in the Civil War.

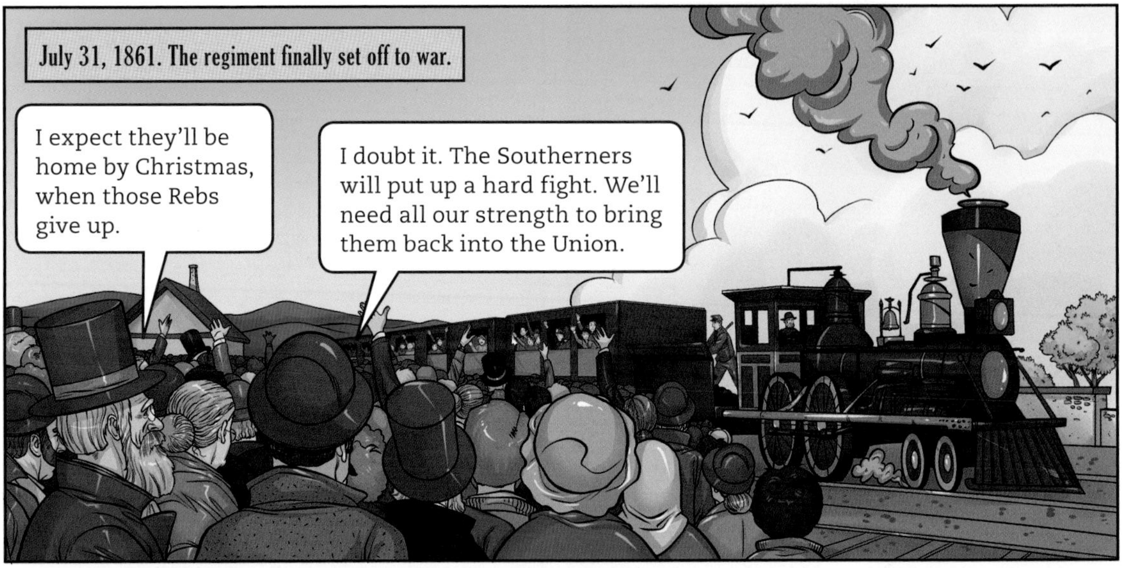
July 31, 1861. The regiment finally set off to war.
I expect they'll be home by Christmas, when those Rebs give up.
I doubt it. The Southerners will put up a hard fight. We'll need all our strength to bring them back into the Union.

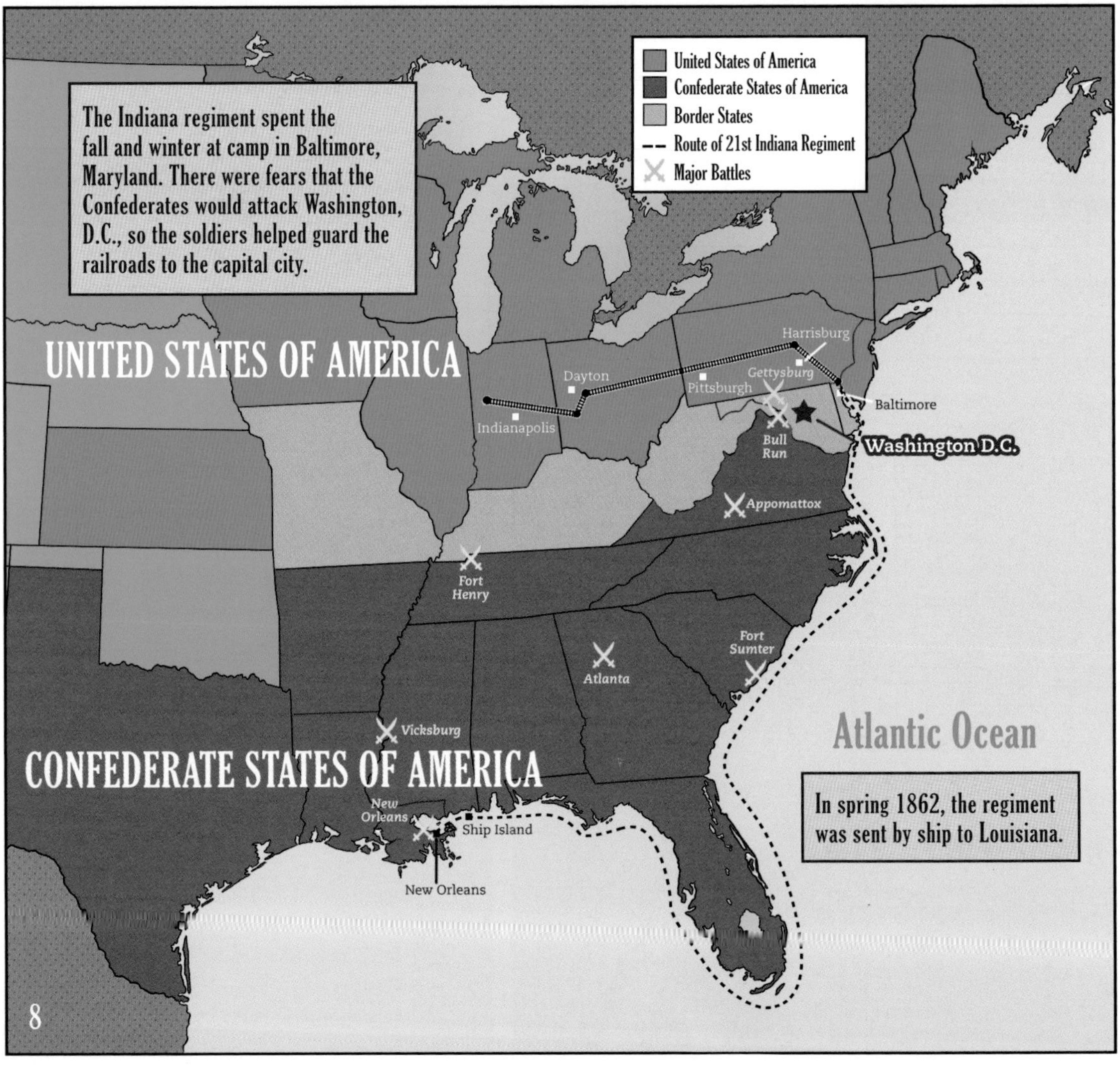
The Indiana regiment spent the fall and winter at camp in Baltimore, Maryland. There were fears that the Confederates would attack Washington, D.C., so the soldiers helped guard the railroads to the capital city.
United States of America
Confederate States of America
Border States
Route of 21st Indiana Regiment
Major Battles
UNITED STATES OF AMERICA
Dayton
Indianapolis
Pittsburgh
Harrisburg
Gettysburg
Baltimore
Bull Run
Washington D.C.
Appomattox
Fort Henry
Fort Sumter
Atlanta
Vicksburg
CONFEDERATE STATES OF AMERICA
New Orleans
Ship Island
New Orleans
Atlantic Ocean
In spring 1862, the regiment was sent by ship to Louisiana.

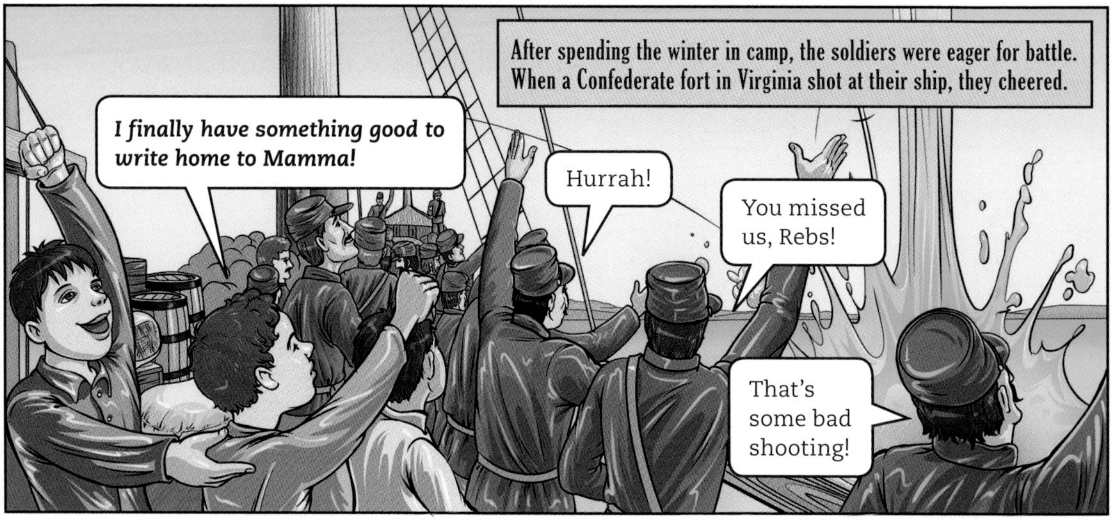
After spending the winter in camp, the soldiers were eager for battle. When a Confederate fort in Virginia shot at their ship, they cheered.
I finally have something good to write home to Mamma!
Hurrah!
You missed us, Rebs!
That's some bad shooting!

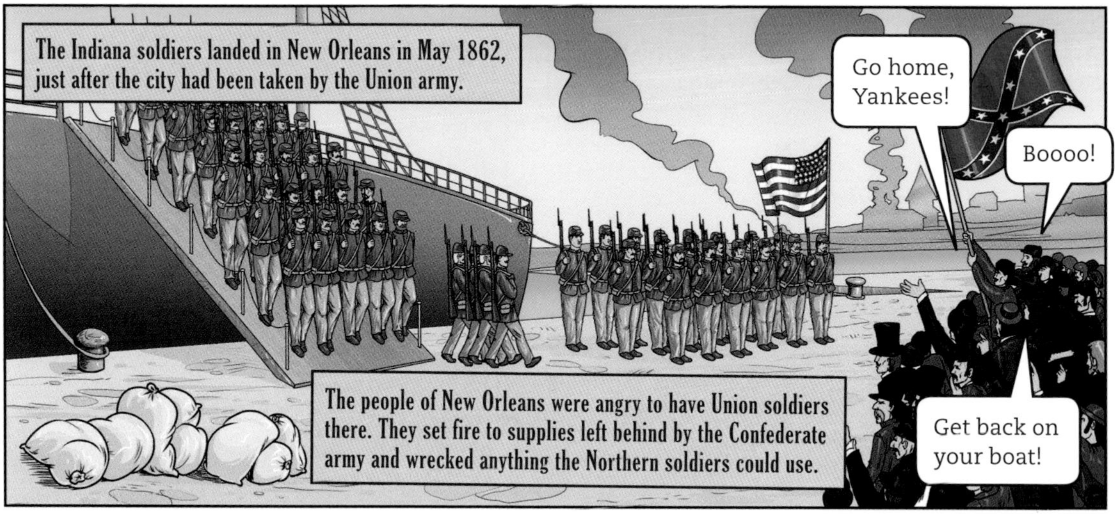
The Indiana soldiers landed in New Orleans in May 1862, just after the city had been taken by the Union army.
Go home, Yankees!
Boooo!
The people of New Orleans were angry to have Union soldiers there. They set fire to supplies left behind by the Confederate army and wrecked anything the Northern soldiers could use.
Get back on your boat!

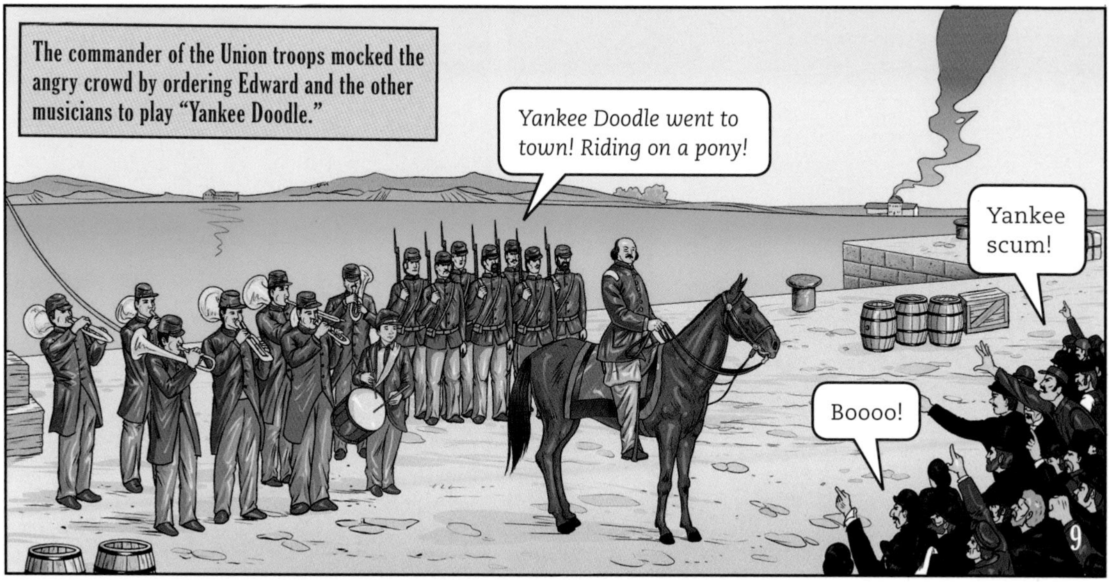
The commander of the Union troops mocked the angry crowd by ordering Edward and the other musicians to play "Yankee Doodle."
Yankee Doodle went to town! Riding on a pony!
Yankee scum!
Boooo!

After a month in New Orleans, the Indiana soldiers and other regiments moved up the Mississippi River to Baton Rouge. The Union generals believed that the Confederates were planning an attack to get the city back.

As in New Orleans, the people of Baton Rouge did not want the Union soldiers there.

They saw the Union troops as an enemy occupation of their city.

Later that summer, the attack came. Edward and the drummer boys had to sound the alarm and wake up the soldiers.

Get up, boys. We need you. The Rebs are coming.

Edward and the other musicians called the troops to order in the early morning.

RUM-PUM-RUM-RUM!

The two armies met outside the city early on the morning of August 5, 1862.

As the lines of soldiers marched to the beat of the drums, they stopped to shoot volleys. They reloaded their muskets, marched forward, and fired again.

Several Union soldiers were wounded or killed by the musket volleys. They retreated to form new lines and fire again.

Fall back! Fall back and regroup!

Can you get up? It's not far back to camp.

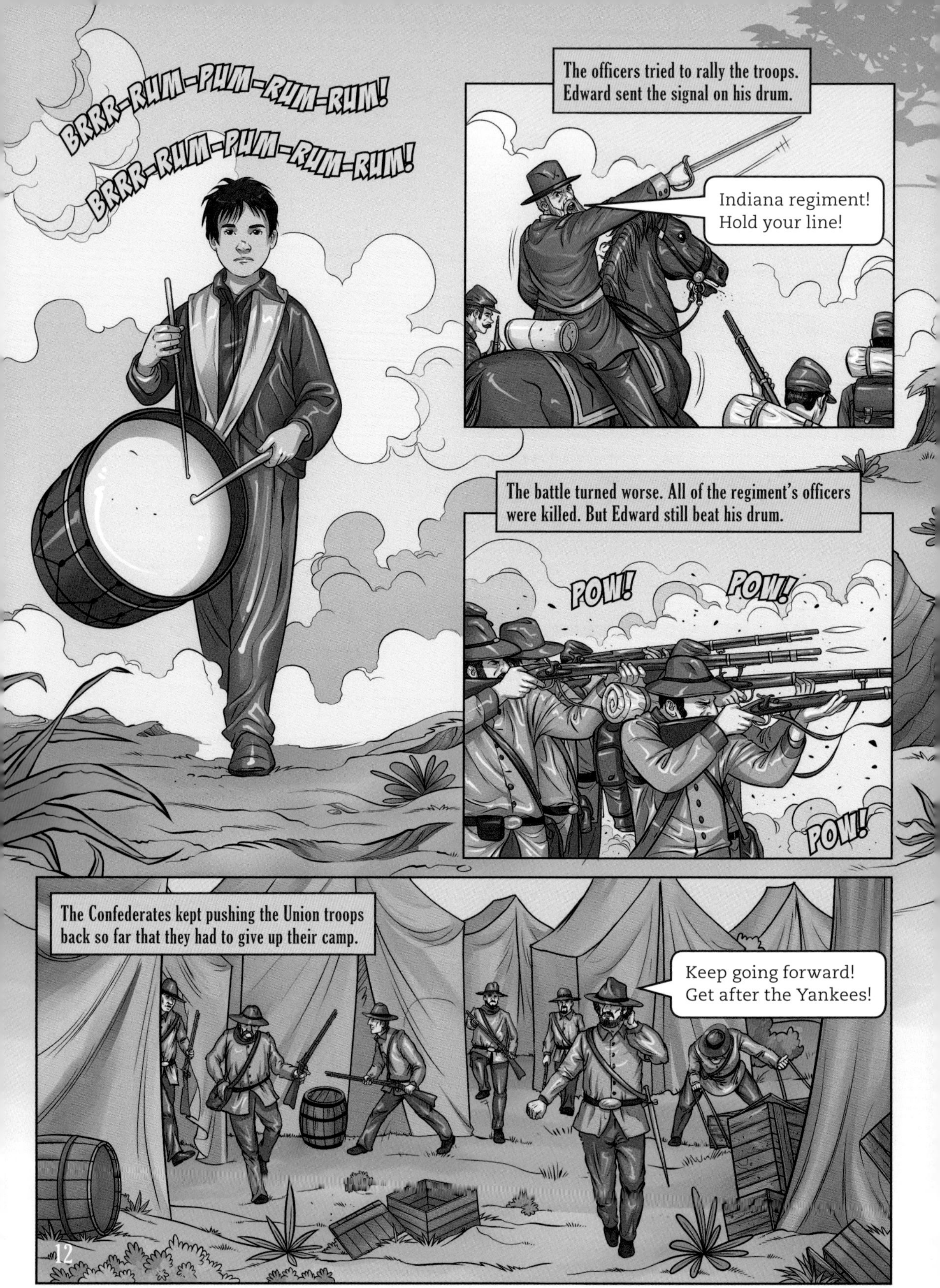
BRRR-RUM-PUM-RUM-RUM!
BRRR-RUM-PUM-RUM-RUM!
The officers tried to rally the troops. Edward sent the signal on his drum.
Indiana regiment! Hold your line!
The battle turned worse. All of the regiment's officers were killed. But Edward still beat his drum.
POW!
POW!
POW!
The Confederates kept pushing the Union troops back so far that they had to give up their camp.
Keep going forward! Get after the Yankees!

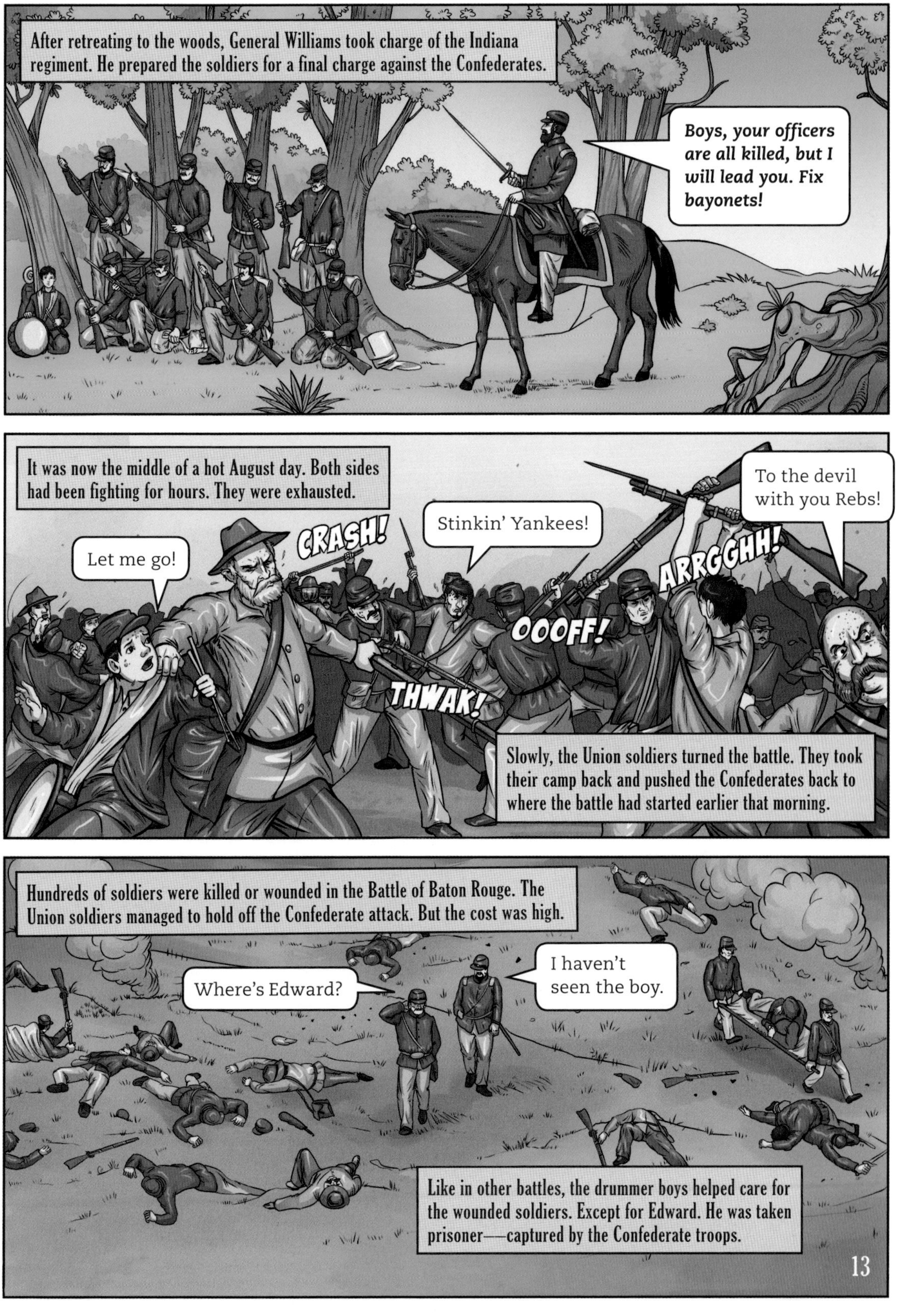
After retreating to the woods, General Williams took charge of the Indiana regiment. He prepared the soldiers for a final charge against the Confederates.
Boys, your officers are all killed, but I will lead you. Fix bayonets!
It was now the middle of a hot August day. Both sides had been fighting for hours. They were exhausted.
Let me go!
CRASH!
Stinkin' Yankees!
To the devil with you Rebs!
ARRGGHH!
OOOFF!
THWAK!
Slowly, the Union soldiers turned the battle. They took their camp back and pushed the Confederates back to where the battle had started earlier that morning.
Hundreds of soldiers were killed or wounded in the Battle of Baton Rouge. The Union soldiers managed to hold off the Confederate attack. But the cost was high.
Where's Edward?
I haven't seen the boy.
Like in other battles, the drummer boys helped care for the wounded soldiers. Except for Edward. He was taken prisoner—captured by the Confederate troops.

Edward Black was not only the youngest soldier to serve in the Civil War. He was also the youngest prisoner of war.

Edward discovered that there were drummer boys on the Confederate side, just like on the Union side.

Where you from, Yank?

I'm from Indiana. Where you from?

We're from Kentucky, just across the river from Indiana.

Why you way down here, fighting us?

Because we have to save the Union. We should be standing together, not fighting each other.

Edward was soon freed when Union troops attacked the camp where he was held prisoner.

Be careful not to hit the prisoners. Those are our boys.

POW!

CRACK!

POW!

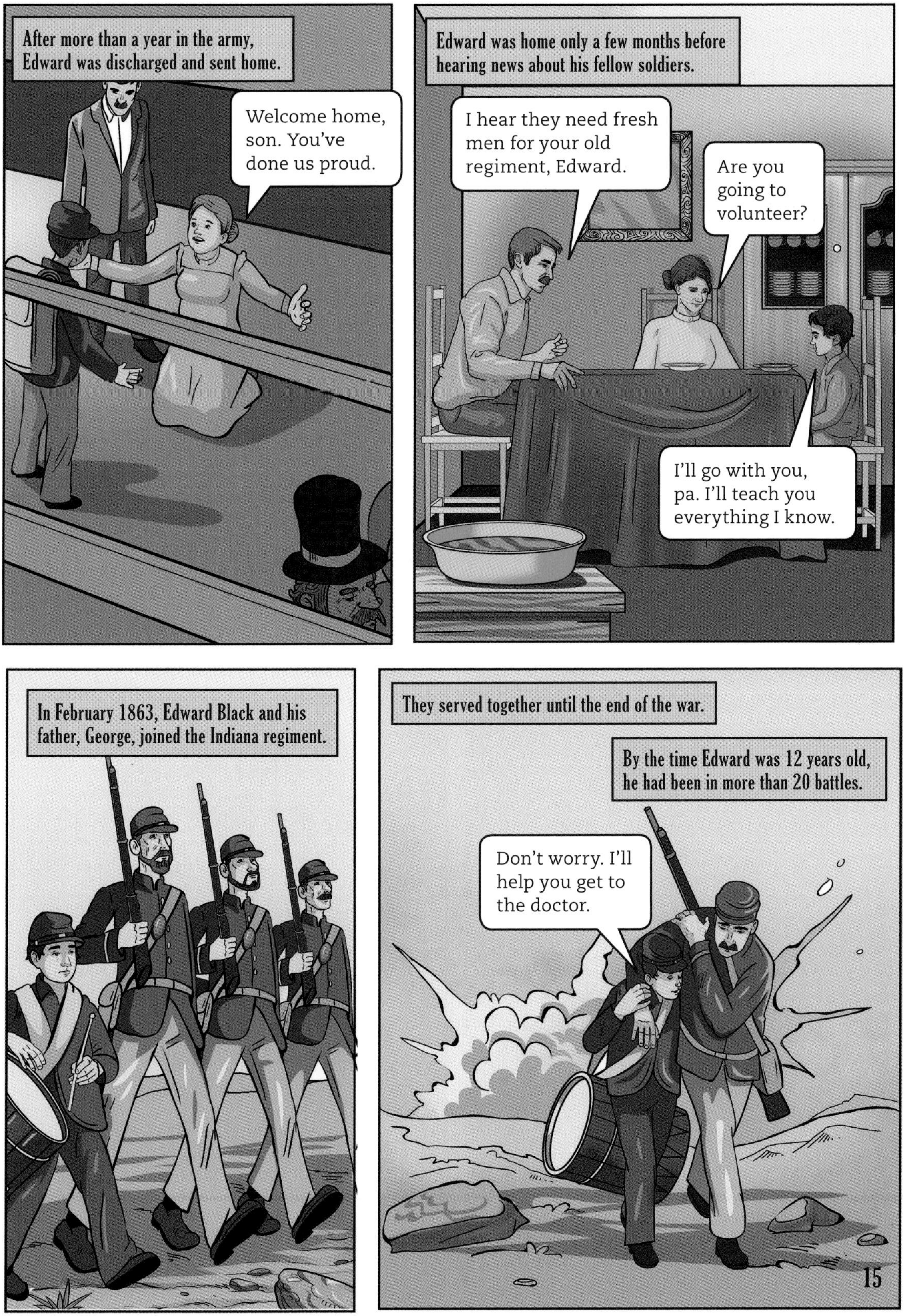
After more than a year in the army, Edward was discharged and sent home.
Welcome home, son. You've done us proud.
Edward was home only a few months before hearing news about his fellow soldiers.
I hear they need fresh men for your old regiment, Edward.
Are you going to volunteer?
I'll go with you, pa. I'll teach you everything I know.
In February 1863, Edward Black and his father, George, joined the Indiana regiment.
They served together until the end of the war.
By the time Edward was 12 years old, he had been in more than 20 battles.
Don't worry. I'll help you get to the doctor.

BROTHERS IN ARMS

Edward Black was not the only boy to serve in the Civil War with his father.

In February 1862, 12-year-old Lyston Howe volunteered to be a drummer boy for the Union army. He joined the 55th Illinois Regiment with his father, William, who led the regimental band.

Lyston's older brother, 14-year-old Orion, had to stay at home.

You're too sick to join them, dear. The strain would be too much for you.

But Orion couldn't stand to be left behind. He soon ran away to join his father and brother.

He sneaked onto a boat carrying goods down the Mississippi River.

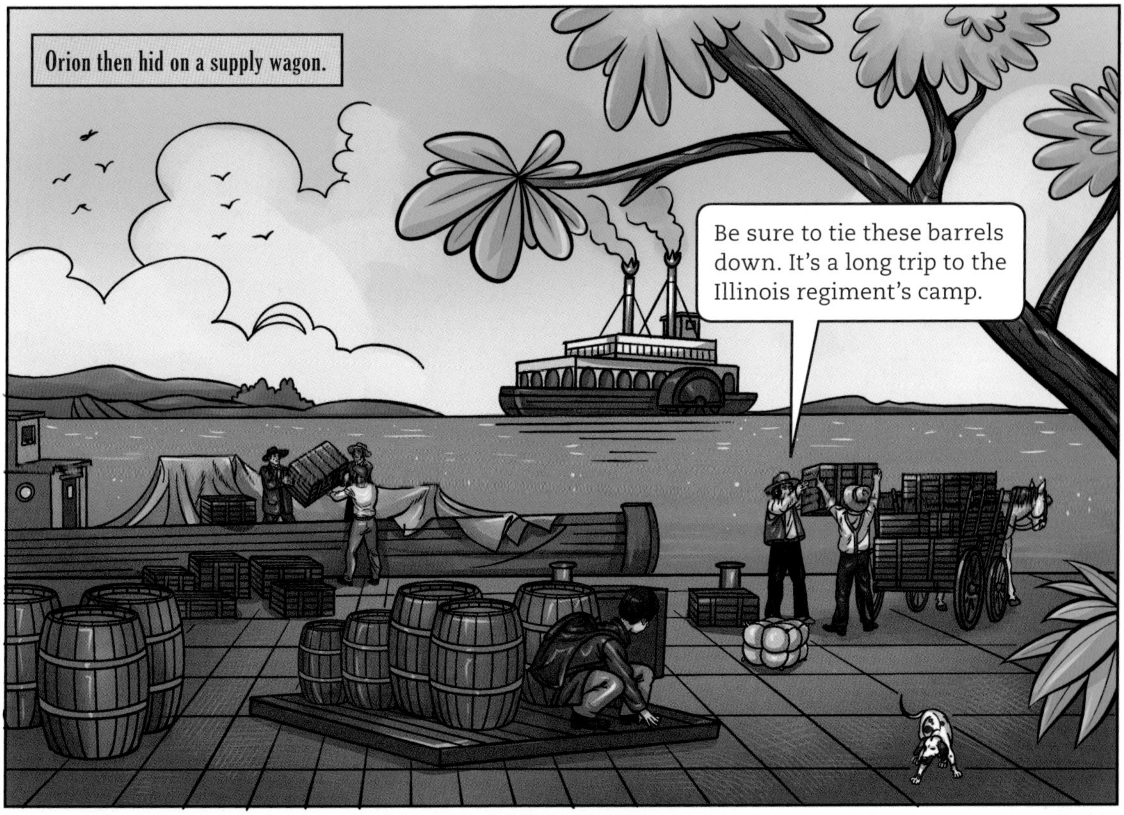
Orion then hid on a supply wagon.
Be sure to tie these barrels down. It's a long trip to the Illinois regiment's camp.

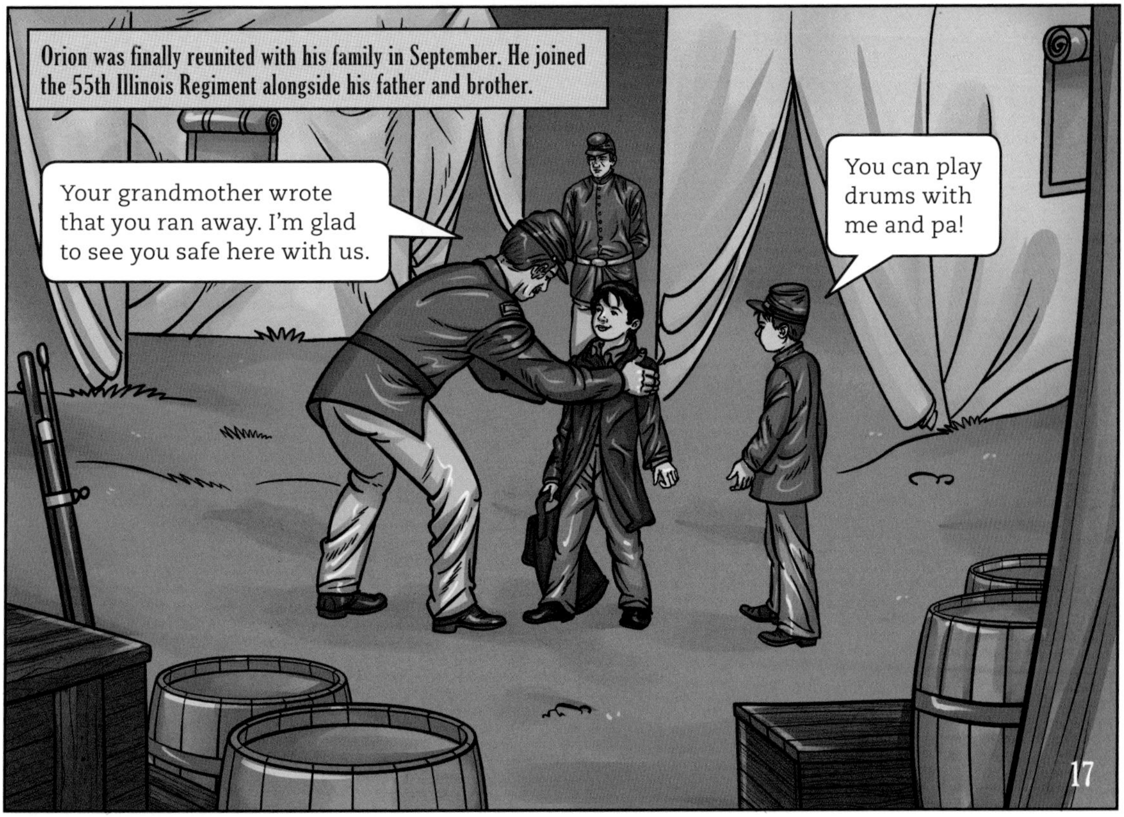
Orion was finally reunited with his family in September. He joined the 55th Illinois Regiment alongside his father and brother.
Your grandmother wrote that you ran away. I'm glad to see you safe here with us.
You can play drums with me and pa!

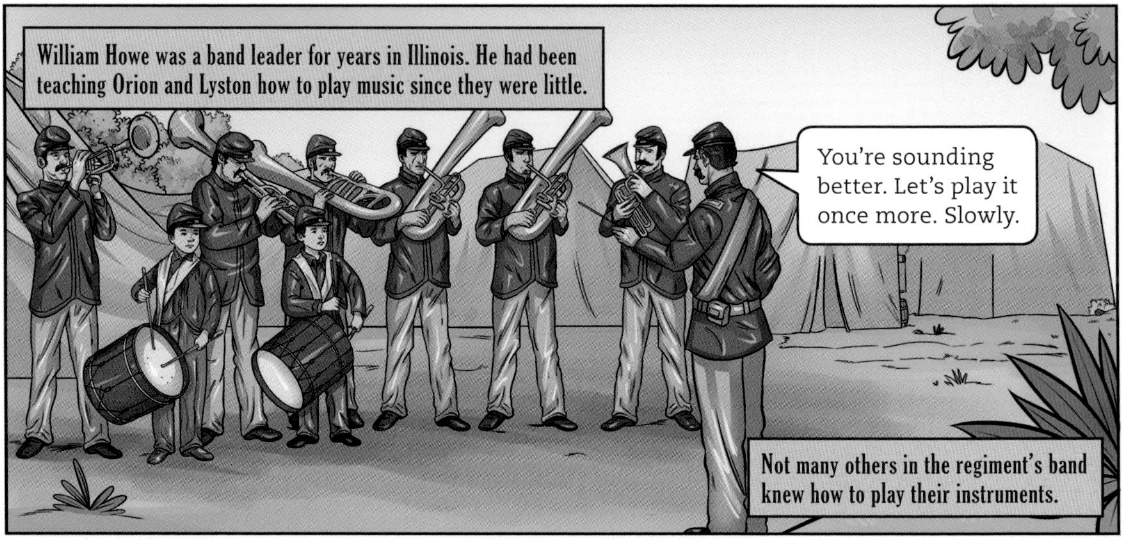
William Howe was a band leader for years in Illinois. He had been teaching Orion and Lyston how to play music since they were little.
You're sounding better. Let's play it once more. Slowly.
Not many others in the regiment's band knew how to play their instruments.

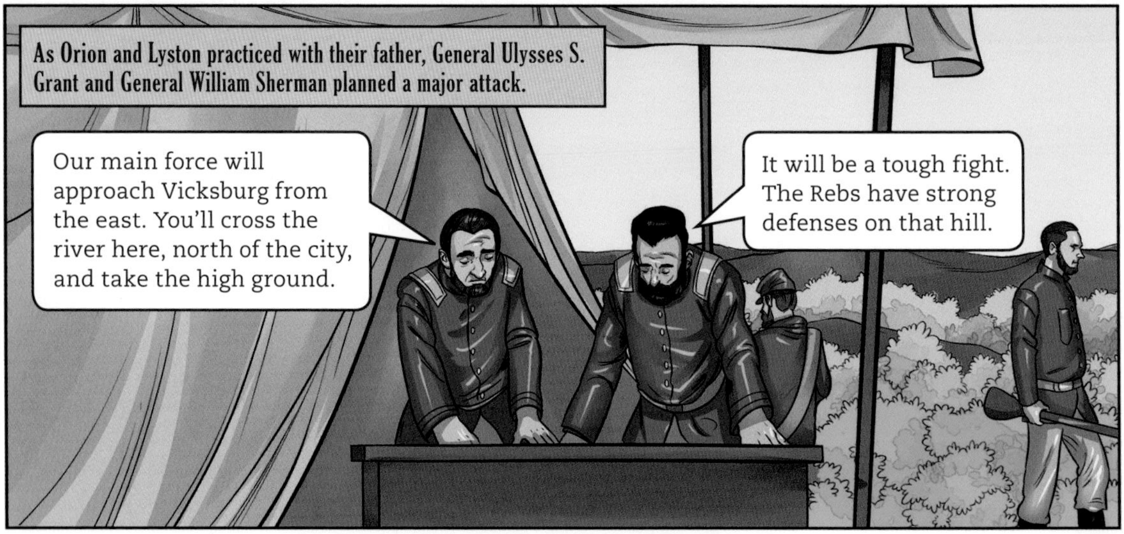
As Orion and Lyston practiced with their father, General Ulysses S. Grant and General William Sherman planned a major attack.
Our main force will approach Vicksburg from the east. You'll cross the river here, north of the city, and take the high ground.
It will be a tough fight. The Rebs have strong defenses on that hill.

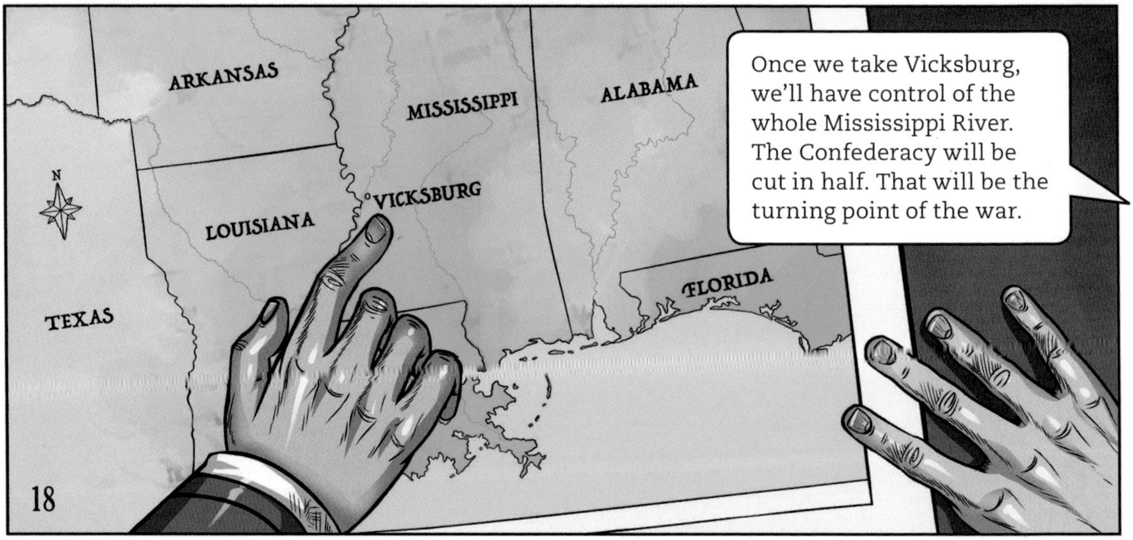
ARKANSAS
MISSISSIPPI
ALABAMA
N
VICKSBURG
LOUISIANA
FLORIDA
TEXAS
Once we take Vicksburg, we'll have control of the whole Mississippi River. The Confederacy will be cut in half. That will be the turning point of the war.

In May 1863, the Union army began its attack on Vicksburg. It would be one of the most important battles of the Civil War.

You boys have to stay behind. This is going to be a hard fight, and we have no need for drummers. You can help with the wounded.

I can't stay here while they're off fighting.

You heard what pa said.

I don't care. I have to help somehow.

Orion found the Illinois regiment on the battlefield. They were trapped by cannon and musket fire from the Confederate side.

And they were running out of cartridges for their own guns.

You need to run back to the general. Tell him we need more cartridges.

Yes, sir!

POW!
POW!
BOOOOOM!
CRACK!
BOOOM!
POW!
POW!
CRACK!
POW!

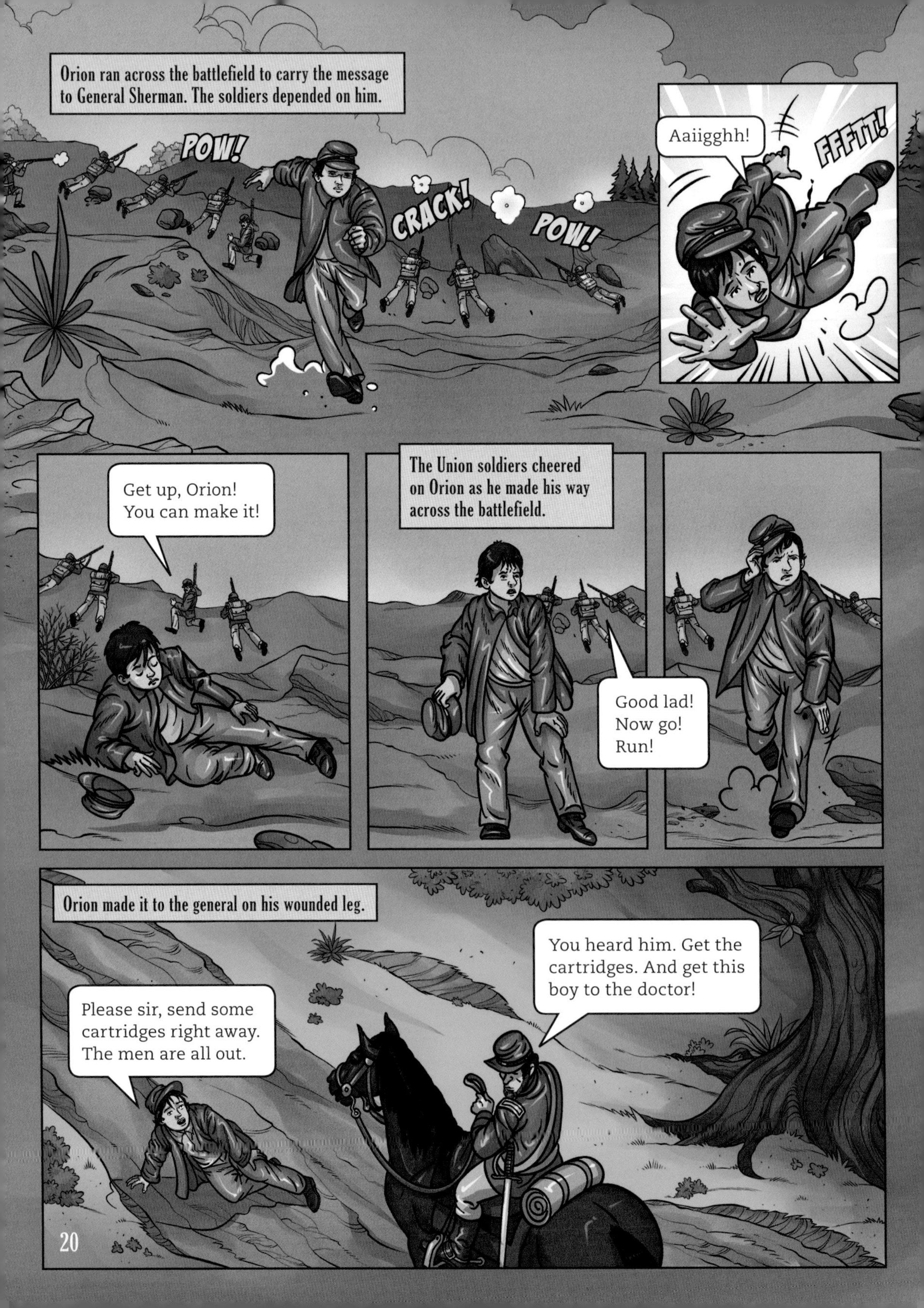
Orion ran across the battlefield to carry the message to General Sherman. The soldiers depended on him.
POW!
CRACK!
POW!
Aaiigghh!
FFFTT!
Get up, Orion! You can make it!
The Union soldiers cheered on Orion as he made his way across the battlefield.
Good lad! Now go! Run!
Orion made it to the general on his wounded leg.
Please sir, send some cartridges right away. The men are all out.
You heard him. Get the cartridges. And get this boy to the doctor!

But even with more cartridges, the Union troops couldn't break through the Confederate lines.

My pa is coming with a stretcher. We'll get you to the hospital.

The generals on both sides agreed to a cease-fire to gather the wounded and dead. Union and Confederate soldiers worked side-by-side to care for their troops.

Later, the Union soldiers kept fighting to take Vicksburg, but the battle was over for Orion.

They said you're going home on the train.

And they might even send you to the academy. You're going to be an officer!

Orion became famous as a war hero. There were newspaper stories and even poems written about him.

Did you read the story about my dear Orion? It says that General Sherman wrote to the Secretary of War himself, recommending him to the academy.

FIGHTING FOR FREEDOM

In the first years of the war, African Americans were not allowed to serve in the Union army. Abraham Lincoln's Emancipation Proclamation later allowed black men to serve as soldiers.

Frederick Douglass, a formerly enslaved black man who became a famous abolitionist, recruited black men in the North to join the army.

The iron gate of our prison is half open. One rush from the North will fling it wide open, and millions of our brothers and sisters will march out in liberty.

In Elmyra, New York, 16-year-old Miles Moore answered the call to serve.

It says there is a regiment for black soldiers forming in Massachusetts.

I can go, Daddy. Massachusetts is a long way. You can't make it with your bad leg.

Miles walked 400 miles (644 kilometers) to volunteer for the 54th Massachusetts Regiment.

You're pretty small to be a soldier.

I work tending horses for the stagecoach. I can handle myself.

We can use you in Company H, even if you're small. We need a drummer boy.

Miles was the same age as some soldiers in Company H. Like many others, he had come from far away to serve in the regiment.

George Brown, from Chicago, Illinois, was 16 years old.

Richard Gomar, age 17, came from Battle Creek, Michigan.

Even the company's commander, Captain Cabot Russell, was only 18 years old.

While all of the soldiers in the 54th Massachusetts were black, the officers were all white.

The 54th regiment was formed in February 1863. That summer, the troops were sent to South Carolina with orders to hold the shoreline.

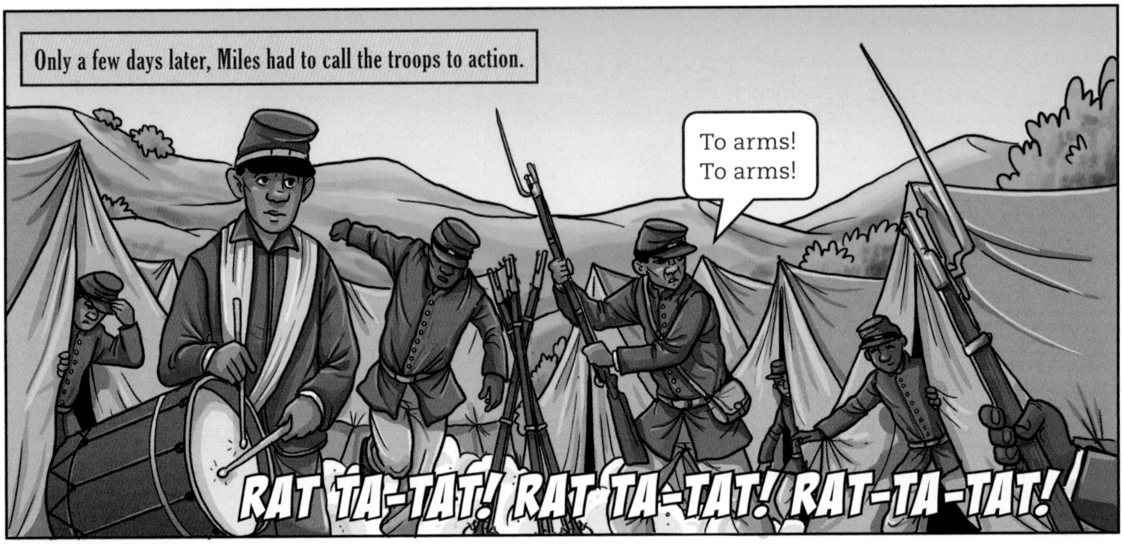
Only a few days later, Miles had to call the troops to action.
To arms! To arms!
RAT TA-TAT! RAT TA-TAT! RAT-TA-TAT!

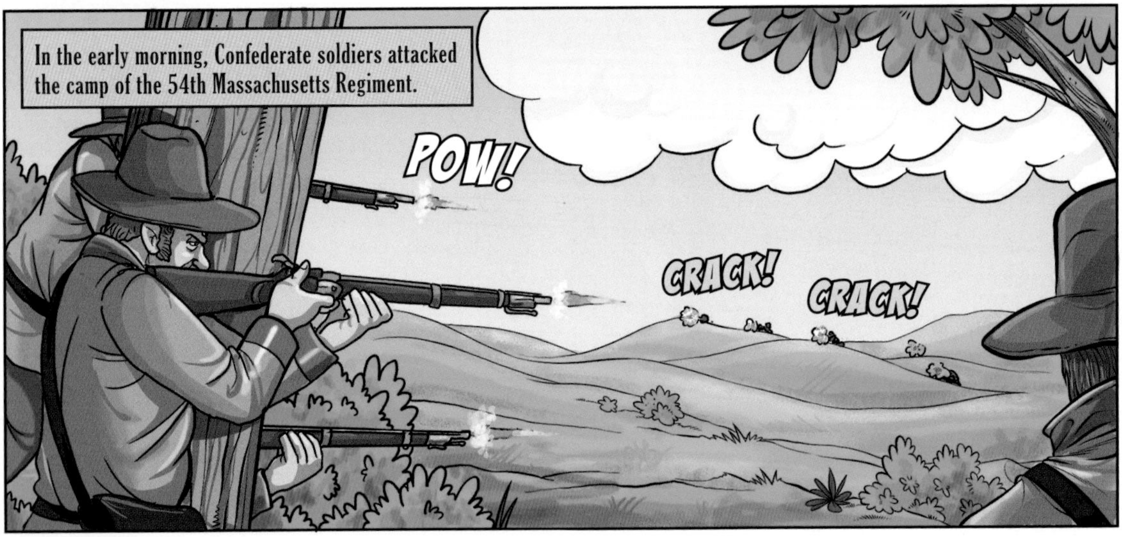
In the early morning, Confederate soldiers attacked the camp of the 54th Massachusetts Regiment.
POW!
CRACK!
CRACK!

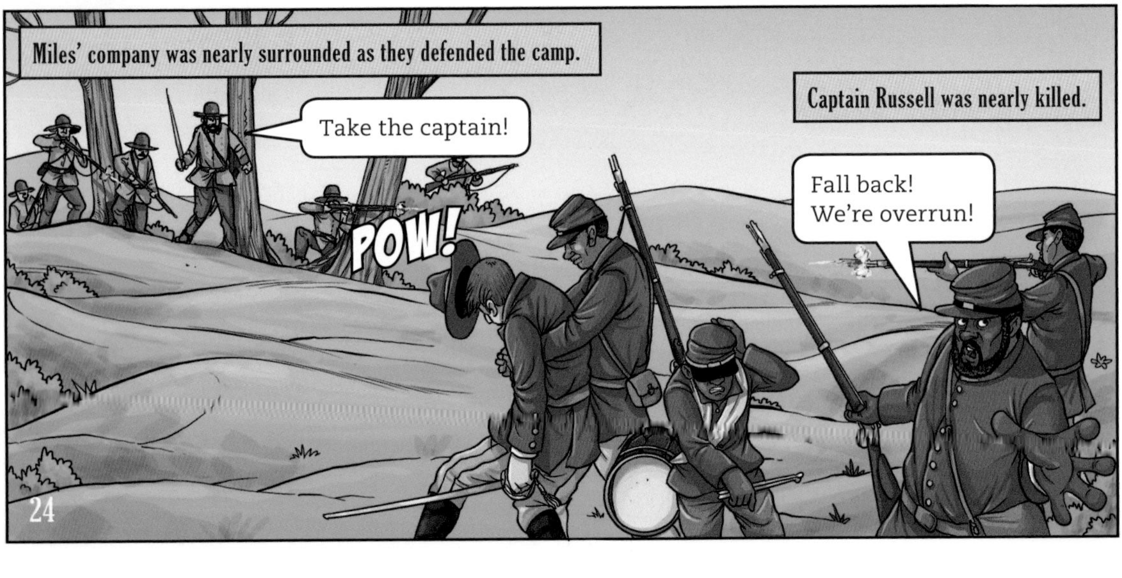
Miles' company was nearly surrounded as they defended the camp.
Take the captain!
POW!
Captain Russell was nearly killed.
Fall back! We're overrun!

Sergeant Wilson held off the Confederates as Company H escaped.

If they capture us, they'll sell us into slavery! Get back to the regiment!

GET BACK! BACK!

Sergeant Wilson was killed holding back the Confederates. Soon after, reinforcements arrived from the Union camp and stopped the attack.

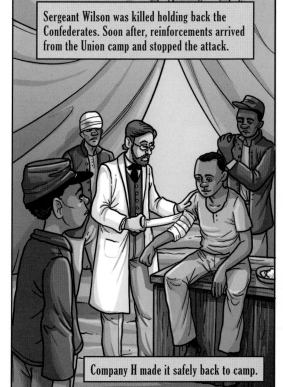

Company H made it safely back to camp.

Company H had shown its courage against the surprise attack. Colonel Shaw, the commander of the 54th Massachusetts Regiment, gave them an important assignment.

Men, you will hold the left flank when we attack Fort Wagner. As long as that fort is in Confederate hands, they control the coast and can fire on our ships.

Two nights later, the 54th Massachusetts Regiment attacked South Carolina's Fort Wagner.

As the Confederate cannons fired overhead, the Union soldiers crept up to the walls.

The Union soldiers made it to the top of the walls. But Captain Russell was hit in the attack. The Confederate soldiers inside the fort then pushed the Union troops off the walls.

As the troops retreated, Miles and the other drummer boys helped the wounded to safety.

After nearly two months of fighting, the Confederates abandoned Fort Wagner. The 54th Massachusetts Regiment moved in to take over.

Miles played his drum as the Union flag was raised over the fort. He served with the regiment in many more battles, until the end of the war.

RETURNING HOME

Throughout the war, hundreds of parents wrote to the government in Washington, D.C., asking for their young sons to be returned home from the army.

Dear Mr. Lincoln,

I ask that you please allow my son, Nathaniel, to return home from the army.

He ran away to serve as a drummer boy when he was 14 years old. Just now, his father has become ill and died.

I am alone on our farm with Nathaniel's younger sisters. We need Nathaniel to help bring in the harvest.

Without him, we will not bring in the grain and the farm will be lost.

Sometimes, the War Department sent parents' letters directly to President Lincoln. In these cases, he always ordered the boys to be released from the army and sent home.

Orion Howe went home after being wounded in battle. He was soon back in the army but was wounded again. He later went to the officers' academy.

But Orion didn't become an officer. He chose a life of adventure instead. He first became a sailor, and he later went out west to work as a cowboy.

After he had finished his adventures, Orion became a dentist. Meanwhile, Lyston Howe opened a hardware store in their hometown.

This is our highest military honor, given in recognition of your heroism at Vicksburg.

Years later, soldiers from the Illinois regiment still remembered Orion's heroic actions. They asked President Grover Cleveland to give him the Medal of Honor. In 1896 Orion went to the White House to receive his award.

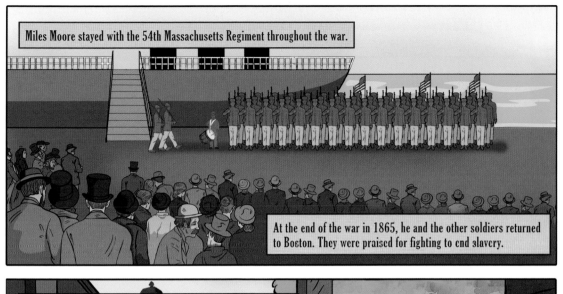

Miles Moore stayed with the 54th Massachusetts Regiment throughout the war.

At the end of the war in 1865, he and the other soldiers returned to Boston. They were praised for fighting to end slavery.

Edward Black and his father also returned from the war in 1865. Their regiment fought in the very last battles of the Civil War.

At just 12 years old, Edward was an experienced veteran. He had seen all of the horrors of war.

Edward was never able to get healthy after the war. He was worn down by all he had seen and done as a child.

Sadly, Edward died when he was only 19 years old. The youngest boy to serve in the Civil War became a casualty of it only a few years later.

GLOSSARY

abolitionist (ab-uh-LI-shuhn-ist)—a person who worked to end slavery

cartridge (KAHR-trij)—a container holding a gun's powder, primer, and bullet

casualty (KAZH-oo-uhl-tee)—someone who is injured, captured, killed, or missing in a war

communications (kuh-myoo-nuh-KAY-shuhns)—messages or information sent between units in the military

discharge (DISS-chahrj)—to relieve or dismiss from service

Emancipation Proclamation (i-MAN-si-pay-shuhn prah-cluh-MAY-shuhn)—a document signed by President Abraham Lincoln during the Civil War that freed enslaved people in Confederate states

flank (FLANGK)—the far left or right side of a group of soldiers or location

musket (MUHSS-kit)—a gun with a long barrel

occupation (awk-yuh-PAY-shuhn)—taking over and controlling an area with military forces

Rebs (REBS)—a nickname for Confederate soldiers during the Civil War

regiment (REJ-uh-muhnt)—a large group of soldiers who fight together as a unit

READ MORE

Ablard, Michelle. *The Civil War: Brother Against Brother.* Huntington Beach, CA: Teacher Created Materials, 2017.

MacCarald, Clara. *Children During the Civil War.* Lake Elmo, MN: Focus Readers, 2019.

Marsico, Katie. *Johnny Clem's Civil War Story.* Minneapolis: Lerner Publications, 2018.

INTERNET SITES

Children During the Civil War
https://www.ducksters.com/history/civil_war/children_during_the_civil_war.php

Children of the Civil War: On the Battlefield
https://www.battlefields.org/learn/articles/children-civil-war-battlefield

The Role of Drummer Boys in the American Civil War
https://www.thoughtco.com/civil-war-drummer-boys-1773732

INDEX